For
Mary Ruth

VER THE RIVER

AND THROUGH THE WOOD

by
Lydia Maria Child

pictures by
Brinton Turkle

SCHOLASTIC INC.

New York Toronto London Auckland Sydney

ISBN 0-590-41190-X

12 11 10 9 8 7 6 5 4 3   9/8 0 1 2/9

Printed in the U.S.A.   08
First Scholastic printing, November 1987

Over the river, and through the wood,
  To grandfather's house we go;

The horse knows the way
To carry the sleigh,
Through the white and drifted snow.

Over the river, and through the wood,
To grandfather's house away!
We would not stop
For doll or top,
For 'tis Thanksgiving Day.

Over the river, and through the wood—
Oh, how the wind does blow!

It stings the toes,
And bites the nose,
As over the ground we go.

Over the river, and through the wood,
With a clear blue winter sky,
The dogs do bark,
And children hark,
As we go jingling by.

Over the river and through the wood,
To have a first-rate play.

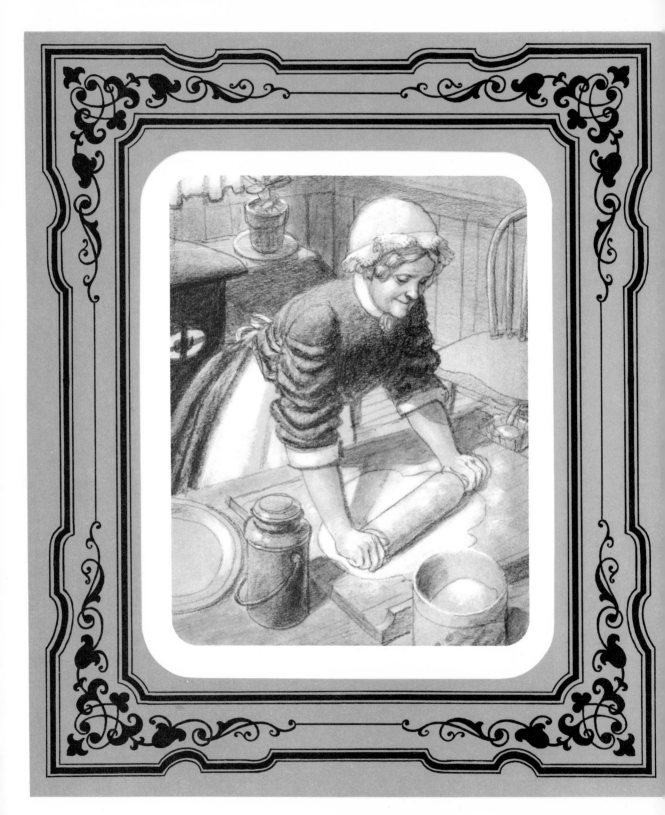

Hear the bells ring,
"Ting-a-ling-ding!"
Hurrah for Thanksgiving Day!

Over the river, and through the wood—
No matter for winds that blow;
Or if we get
The sleigh upset,
Into a bank of snow.

Over the river, and through the wood,
To see little John and Ann;

We will kiss them all,
And play snowball,
And stay as long as we can.

Over the river and through the wood
Trot fast my dapple-gray!
Spring over the ground
Like a hunting-hound!
For this is Thanksgiving Day.

Over the river and through the wood,
And straight through the barnyard gate.

We seem to go
Extremely slow—
It is so hard to wait!

Over the river, and through the wood—
Old Jowler hears our bells;
He shakes his pow,
With a loud bow-wow,
And thus the news he tells.

Over the river, and through the wood—
When grandmother sees us come,

She will say, "Oh, dear,
The children are here,
bring a pie for every one."

Over the river and through the wood—
Now grandmother's cap I spy!
Hurrah for the fun!
Is the pudding done?
Hurrah for the pumpkin-pie!

OVER THE RIVER